Apricity

Anushka Singh

 pencil

Apricity

ISBN 978-93-5458-946-1

Published in India 2021 by Pencil

A brand of

One Point Six Technologies Pvt. Ltd.

123, Building J2, Shram Seva Premises,

Wadala Truck Terminal, Wadala (E)

Mumbai 400037, Maharashtra, INDIA

E connect@thepencilapp.com

W www.thepencilapp.com

DISCLAIMER: *The opinions expressed in this book are those of the authors and do not purport to reflect the views of the Publisher.*

Author biography

Anushka is a twenty year old residing in the captital of India. She is a published author with two seperate anthologies already in the market. Anushka is a commerce student but her interest lies deeply in weaving words together.This is her first individual book. She believes that anyone can write , what takes it to become an art is passion. She writes her mind on her instagram handle as well i.e wizardry_writings.

CONTENTS

Introduction

I have been writing poems, musings, observations and my epiphanies in my diary since a long time. To be honest, this book is a way to tame some of those scattered thoughts inside one safe place. There are poetries, open letters and even short stories in this tiny book of mine. I really hope anyone who reads it shares a moment of intimacy with the thoughts presented inside it. I have given this book some of my best collective write ups, and to share them with all of my readers is a matter of immense joy for me.

I will not take pages to welcome you all inside my head . I have written a whole book for you to prepare a judgement.

I wish for each one of you to have a relatable read.

Tables of Content

Poems I scribbled

A few Snippets from the way I see the world

Poems I scribbled

The days which still have a part of me

The sand, the dust,

the swing untouched.

The days of rainbows,

examples of current angst.

The silver beads of merry days,

days of dirt with actual clay.

wingless flights, insane sanity,

not a touch of harmful reality.

Empty sky, droplets of rain,

weren't lover's tears spent in vain.

Hope to dream again tomorrow,

was unasked, not a wish out of sorrow.

New faces weren't always home,

seldom check-ups where the heart romes.

With each day spent, I grew up a bit,

killing insides of mine, the happy kid.

Poor Tale of Fortune

Another week gone, the armchair untouched,

Quiet doormat, eager to embrace any foreign feet.

Home sends for me, again this time

couldn't reach to me, again this time.

Families recollecting memories together,

This day feels lonelier than for ever.

Sweets, flowers, door-balconies dressed of lights,

Never have I even celebrated this festival, I cried

my poor heart doesn't know the boundaries at all,

Emptiness doesn't ask, Diwali or Eid's fate stall.

My bank balance mocks my expressions,

For what is this money, in a helpless situation.

Poor Tale of Fortune

Another week gone, the armchair untouched,

Quiet doormat, eager to embrace any foreign feet.

Home sends for me, again this time

couldn't reach to me, again this time.

Families recollecting memories together,

This day feels lonelier than for ever.

Sweets, flowers, door-balconies dressed of lights,

Never have I even celebrated this festival, I cried

my poor heart doesn't know the boundaries at all,

Emptiness doesn't ask, Diwali or Eid's fate stall.

My bank balance mocks my expressions,

For what is this money, in a helpless situation.

Colorless widow

I see red, capes and shawls.

My fichu is colorless, I'm falling as fall.

Hair untied not because of wind,

my hair is gone, they have been declared as a sin.

Roses, marigold, fresh leaves on my floret

Stinks in a corner, scum, tears wet

The jingling of bangles once painted forehead

Tales of misfortune now brings you a dread.

A walking reminder, mornings are difficult

I didn't die with him, is that an insult?

Regular death happening in bits,

He died once; it was a one-time smit.

Why is my sky pale now?

Whom do I ask this?

I died when he left

Why do I have to wail again?

Daily?

Escape

I was afraid actually terrified,

I knew it then but my mother lied.

I was ten, unaware of truth or reality,

What she faced was beyond humanity.

I remember silent cries from that room,

The next day, she couldn't hold the broom.

She said papa loved her that's why he craved,

But all he did was using marriage to cover rapes.

The night she screamed, I ran to her,

She was standing still, blood all over.

23

I don't remember when was I this happy,

The blood was not of my mother but of my daddy.

A routine end

He comes to lay beside the seashore

With thoughts of hate and heinous crimes

A mind of ruthless routine,

a heart rusting alone, a coal mine

The world seems quiet to him.

When he sees the ocean waving back

for one time he realizes

silence isn't always too bad!

Again, he reaches to hold the pistol lying beside him

It's tough he feels, but somehow comforting him.

A seagull watches him, observes his every move

The man thinks of days when the seashore wasn't this mute.

The pistol lies there as he walks inside the sea

The wetness of the hem of his pants reaches upwards to kiss his lips.

Finally, his head is under the world of worries and doles,

The seagull can finally fly away,

his only friend has gathered the peace he deserved.

A celebration of death

What will happen to her if he jumps today?

The squirrels will ask each time he'll get to the mountain top.

For every time he reaches there and stand to decide the wind,

The trees make fun of him

Challenging his strength, the will to kill.

His wife will again come, calling him names and tear-filled eyes

Again, the baby will cry as his father will be brought back to life,

For what is this crying, for a corpse who's living,

The world will die, the world will live,

The wife will crave but the human will be released.

The birds flapped their wings as fast they could,

The wife was late today, the man finally stood.

A satisfied smile was passed among the flies.

Daisy

What are those petals for, I ask?

Draping the leaf around her stem, she stood straight to show me herself.

A white daisy is what they call her,

For me, she's just my mother.

Sunlight was too bright,

the wind making me sway

My mother in her shine,

 in her blooming state.

Stay close to your friends,

she yelled at me, suddenly

What was the hurry?

There she was gone being grabbed by a bully.

Men will treat us the way they want

This doesn't mean I'll lower my charm

Words of my daisy still pours my heart to melt,

For what are these hands to do

When I'm nowhere to end.

Today when I lay thinking about women,

A daisy again is being snatched

Being crushed under the sky.

Only if they knew, I'm a daisy too.

She wasn't the last one to live

She won't be the last to die too.

Mockery

The lunch box which stayed inside always

Is now lying flat on the ground,

The one face who loved being not watched,

Is gathering audience from every floor.

Was he not a brilliant scholar?

Someone says in the crowd

The books mock them silently,

If they knew, only if they knew.

With his face pasted to the ground,

His skull parted in two

United shoelaces kept neatly beside him

And an ink pen broken, liquid blue.

Whose child is this, a man of responsibility asks

whatever does it matter

whose existence is really to be asked.

Finally, someone laughs, someone to do something

sane

The laugh was from the notebook

The papers which his hand held.

A beautiful story was written on them

Of a boy with sadness

Of a boy who needed help.

Every time they read them now,

 he smiles again

Only if they did before

Only if they knew; asked.

Comfort at last

It all came at once,

The screeching noises, the hands choking breath
out of my lungs.

The long tedious routines of walks,

the same kitchen counter again.

The same sky watching me, mocking my existence.

Not for once it stopped,

the continuous longing of breeze on my bones.

My flesh is not feeling anything anymore, I need it
to be ripped in parts,

it to feel how cold my nose used to get.

I want to do that today, in this comfort.

The comfort of dying in your arms, in my arms.

I see you. I promise.

When you sit under the autopsy of your own dreams. You realize how much of how many things you have accomplished without paying attention. And how much of you is still alive, without your dead faith.

What keeps you alive? Is what I am asking.

There is someone, something or even a moment maybe. Which makes you want to breathe a little more. Was it good to continue even after you thought you died with your hopes? You tell me that. Not always we find sources to live.

To be born, how easy it is. You do not put any efforts in it.

But to live? How courageous it is to live.

It is okay to let go. Not everyone is brave, I understand it.

But for when you were brave, I appreciate you.

I appreciate myself.

So should you. Live for that moment of reflection.

Or die for it.

That is the power you have.

Not your dead aspirations.

Love

I caught myself wondering,

Not about you,

 but about the path.

The path which was ours

The bench under the tree

Where we used to meet,

after three.

Now with us gone

Is it also lonely like me?

Is there someone to count the bricks of the wall?

Or was our name the last on it.

The flowers still grow pink

Or the beauty has faded?

The wind blows freely,

Or are there faces on its way?

The leaves still crack when stepped on

Or they too have learnt to be quiet in pain?

I caught myself wondering,

Not about you, but about the path.

A Beach Story

She walks by without failing to gather,

Gather my attention and grab my heart.

A blue sky paints my skyline

when her scarf rubs off her impressions.

I wish she wouldn't do it again,

Leave your prints for me to walk on.

My heart scares me, beats too fast,

Will my hand ever hold hers?

I ask her, today I finally do

The red on her face, pushes me to assume.

Her fingers are shivering, is she nervous?

I step back, maybe I assumed wrong.

This is what she wrote for me.

I tell our toddler, again this time,

Having her in my arms,

And my scarf is still a source of jealousy.

For You

For you

Every time the sun rises

I find myself wondering,

about the comfort

this heat provides,

Is it really the dawn which pulls me?

Or the warmth of your presence

Of your mere existence.

Again.

There is a brief moment when

everything makes sense,

 I think your name is that

moment of my life.

your smile isn't the source of

comfort for me

It is a place of safety,

As if, your face

radiates sunshine,

Creates the dawn,

How surprising,

How mesmerizing.

Forever.

In the end, my love just glorifies my aches

Hope of peace and lacking of grace.

The jar holds all of me in there,

Scattered emotions, out growing despair.

Plenty of water wasted in reminiscing you,

What would it take to bury, to drown in you?

Swallowed

I seek for a shadow to escape from my own,

A long-lost day of sprints

Of huffing paradise in dreams,

I stay under a foreign shadow

To erase whole of mine.

Consume my existence

this time I desire it,

There isn't enough smoke for me

To hide inside, today.

After all, I am bleeding

For my existence to stay

My moon

If I could fly to the stars, I would still not

The moon brings heights and my heart suggests it's wrong.

My moon is still here with me,

Those eyes gather dreams and whistles of everything happy this earth has.

The curling paws which leave impression of dust on my sweater

The same sweater which had no value before meeting him, meeting my moon.

World isn't as easy as my moon sees it,

But somehow, he convinces me,

He makes me want to solve it.

Was it really a coincidence which led you to me?

whatever was the reason.

I'm grateful,

for whatever reasons

I'm grateful.

A few Snippets from The way I see the world.

A Treat of Past

The grass feels much softer than what I remember. From the past years I had always wanted to come back and look at myself from this place. These exact spot-on which millions of incidents happened in my life which shaped me into what I am today. The garden is not just beautiful but it is too pretty to my little heart. Feels like yesterday when I was running away here and there with my siblings in this backyard. Siblings. One of the most complicated but easy relationships that I have experienced in my life. My heart fills with so much joy when I look back at the moments which I spent with my sister in this house. This reminds me of an incident, stay with me and I will tell you the sweetest memories of my life. Memories always fetch memories; I hope yours are attentive enough. It was my fourth birthday; I remember being excited for the party which was planned for the evening. Too excited that I tripped twice that day. As any child of my age, I was really looking forward to my presents. I clearly remember asking for a toy barbie doll from my parents. They agreed, why wouldn't they. That day on 16 July, my birthday party happened, my friends came and oh so many balloons. A house filled with warm snacks and crispy wafers. The only missing part of that day was my parents. They were at the hospital because apparently my sister was very competitive when it came to seeking attention. Of all the days in the year, she chose my birthday to be hers. When my parents came back from the hospital, my silly younger self asked for the present that I had asked for. My mother with her bright face and tired body looked at me as if I were the most amusing creature she had ever seen, except the little baby she held in her arms. My arms wide open and eyes filled with anticipation pushed my mother to, slowly, very slowly put the baby in my arms. With the racing heart of a four-year-old elder sister I then and there declared her to be my barbie. Barbie, the most beautiful child that I had ever seen obviously because I couldn't remember my own face.

Since that day, I have always and obviously shared my birthday with her. We cut cakes together and I love it too much to let go. The grass eventually makes you feel relaxed, doesn't it? The soft touch of twigs combining with the naked soul of my foot makes me feel so much and nothing. It reminds me of the little things that can make anyone feel at peace. This house is not just a home but a memory lane for me. A memory which can make me feel like I have just been wrapped in a cosy blanket after having my winter night bath. It was a routine in our home. You know, to skip early morning bathing, Delhi winters are too much for small children. My ride to school was mostly filled with curious questions from Barbie and yes, my brother.

My brother is the youngest of us, I remember his tiny hands held in mine while crossing the roads. He would always tuck to my hand so tightly and on the other side, my sister would try to run after escaping my grip. She was a very naughty child, my sister and the smallest one fell in the pampered category. Which me and my sister still secretly envy. We all went to the same school and being the elder sister there were many times when I had to solve their silly quarrels. Our father used to give us a few bucks to have a treat after school and my siblings would take chances on who would get my share this time. Because I did not like snacking sometimes and they were more into it than I was. These two are the most annoying yet my favorite people in the whole world. Some relationships feel like gazing at the sky, it is beautiful and so out of reach.

So complicated if we get into details but amazingly gorgeous when stared at for hours.

Today at my wedding ceremony, both of my favorite faces are somewhere running some errands for the event. And here I am living all those moments again and sitting peacefully, that is what pleasure it gives to be an elder sibling.

Parenthood and my observations

Often, we hear people complaining about being born. People who say that their parents were selfish in bringing them in this world. Which makes me think about the reasons, the reasons of how I am at all a source of quenching their thirst of selfishness. Is it just another excuse of mine? Because as always, we are looking for an escape from reality. To lean on and to blame. Parents, humans, are not imperfect. They are normal and they are full of flaws but they get mistaken and forget this. In the process of becoming ideal for their kids, they forget basic human rules, being wrong, doing mistakes, empathy, at times. Children look up to their parents, they are the one source of everything for their kids, and children treat their parents as gods. And as naive as humans are, parents start to believe it. They start to accept each prayer of worship poured on them from their innocent child. Becoming a parent is not a door of entering superiority but a journey of learning all over again.

~ Children are innocent they say, they don't have any worries we believe, but what we don't realize is that what makes them that way, the lack of pride in accepting their faults, the absence of egoistic poking in their back of heads and the understanding of facts which they know they lack in. Children accept the truth of being incapable of knowing it all, they understand that there is a lot more in this world to learn which they don't know and that is what makes them carefree. The biggest mistake we do as adults is that start believing that we know all of it. That brings clusters of issues in our lives. The doors to knowledge should never be closed, perfection of a being is just a window to seek, we can't pass through.

Is it a Trauma

I was just a child when I had to give up a sport I really liked. I don't know if it happens near you too or is it just my neighborhood story.

A story where parents make their children join things that they think are good for their kids, things like abacus classes, things like sports.

They send you away to build you, they put you in classes, summer camps which you start with hating them and then as soon as you are into it. They fetch you away, they snatch you away from that because then you have no time to focus on studies. Which again is something that parents want.

I had to join skating classes when I was twelve or maybe eleven, I do not remember.

Hot summer days, on my skates I used for flow like water, I loved it. The speed, the freedom, I loved their decision of putting me there but it was just until they without considering my opinion dropped me off from my classes. They bought me a cycle, they said cycling is better for me now, for me? Or for them to say out loud. I don't remember. As I said I was young, a kid.

I remember cycling to the place where my skating classes would take place, my friends waving goodbyes and hellos to me. My instructor saying, he missed me. All of that I still have in my mind but it isn't something I feel like talking about. It is not a trauma, is it?

Do you feel sad for me? Funny.

I don't feel sad, I feel so many things but not anger. I feel I wanted them to let me do my skating, to let me be a person what I wanted to be at an age of eleven.

When you are a child, you think of your parents as people who are always right. You trust your parents so much that you even tell your pinky promises to them. You tell how Sharon from 1 D pisses in her pants and pretends she didn't do it.

You even accidentally, just accidentally eat chocolates from kitchen cabinet without telling mommy. Later on, you are giggling about it with her.

When do you change from being a baby to being treated as a baby?

You are really keen on being my friend that you are still reading it. You are a person with a choice to not read but you are still here, I am amused.

I have realized, how we as children make our parents believe in their supremacy, how we blindly keep adding in their pride and how we make them self-obsessed entities.

We do not do it deliberately; we don't even realize that we are doing it just until it starts harming us.

The funniest thing is that they enjoy it, they start believing in their child's assumptions and they start carrying a load of pretentious perfection on their backs. How can I admit that my decision of sending my kid to boarding was wrong and selfish? How can I accept the fact that I hate when my twenty-year-old son tries to throw his opinion at me, but only if it doesn't match mine? Wouldn't this be funny if I allow myself to feel guilty of things that I've done for my kids? All these questions are just reflections of how a parent mind works, mostly.

Well, you would not know or let me guess, do you?

Will you write one thing that you wish your parents didn't do to you, which they believed was for your benefit?

Come on, give it a thought.

A Question which keeps me grounded

Are you, with all due respect, obligated to take all the kind privileges that they offer you with? Think. Question yourself. And when in the poor state of self-realization, with whatever you realize. Start to ponder on the mistakes forgiven. Your parents are not perfect, they are humans. They have been grown up in this sweet sacred prison of societal norms that now they can't differentiate between themselves and supremely valued legendsI won't use big words. I will just keep saying things in simple terms. In terms, like these. Using endearments, saying sorry, confessing love. All of these are just a part of life and death.

Just like mistakes.

Just like people who perform mistakes. Just like
people who forgive.
Just like you and just like me.
Like your mother and like my
father.

I will not ask you to reminisce in sacred honey of
past, gardens of flowers and when life was not so
difficult. But instead, I will just ask you to breathe
and remember that always, and always remember
to forgive.

They might trigger you; you might even feel like
killing the feeling, the ache. How can she hurt me
like that, she is my mother for God's
sake?
Well that most certainly explains how she can hurt
you. Is she allowed to hurt you? I will not comment

on that.If a friend of mine says something devastating to me, it's contagious for my body. I feel like my body is numb. My mind is so calm that I can't process anything but is she allowed to do that? Who allows anyone to hurt us?

No one does. It happens. That's how world works. You get hurt and you, only you can understand if it is worth or not. It is you who will decide if they want to devour themselves in the pool of sorrows or not.So, to answer this question. It is not your mother who gets the question of hurting you, because, your mother, above all is a human. A human who is not perfect and can, most likely will again, hurt your feelings.So instead of feeling sad about the fact that she, being your mother hurt you. Start scribbling under the understanding that being hurt from your own family, from your own parents is most certainly the loveliest thing to absorb, while being a human.

A father like mine

I have never seen him sad; he says he has no problems. When I asked him about my fees, he said my work was to study. I asked him about his life, he told me things which he suffered through but I never felt any of those things to touch me because he never let it happen to me. He left his home when he was fifteen years old, he left his parents - my grandparents, at his house to follow his future. He was working hard because he wanted to have a security of his future. His future, me, he worked hard for me. He slept nights without a single fan on the roof, he was not rich, he was poor. We have three air conditioners in our house. He said he lived alone, cooked food which was barely edible not because he couldn't afford but because he was a child, he did not know how to cook. He smiles telling all this to me, he says he had worked hard for me to smile. I love him. I love my father. I don't know when will he tell me about his issues. Never, I guess because for him I am still a child which he has to protect. I have done nothing in my life for him, I have just taken him for granted. I have never seen any messages that he sends me, he sends me videos of new invented machineries which they forward on social sites, I ignore him. Never have responded. He tells me about his dreams and I hear him with an urge of him to stop. He speaks English with me and I smile knowing his efforts, he says he wished he knew how to form poetries like me. He doesn't understand what I write but he still smiles and tell me they're good. Never in my life have I seen him saying he is done; he has done enough for me but his definition of enough equals to infinity. I am here writing this when he has gone to office, he has zero idea I am here pouring my heart out with my vision blurred with tears. One day I will show this to him, when he will smile and give me an appreciation which I won't be deserving. I know he will say I've written a good piece but he won't say that I've written him. He won't admit that I have told you all about him. He is shy. He is my father.

My Daughter gets me

I walked anxiously to the nurse, I didn't know what to say and the feelings inside of my heart were different. I was filled with emotions, emotions which I have never easily poured out, emotions which escalated to the brim of my moist eyes when I held you in my arms. A tiny baby in my hands, a baby which I knew was mine. After exact four years I got to experience that again, I was blessed with a girl again but now I wasn't naive enough to think that this world is as peaceful as your innocence. I could not be as carefree as I used to be. I started to care, more than you think was okay. I did things, I made rules and I kept you safe. That was my idea of keeping you safe. No, I never discriminated, I never loved you both even an ounce less than I should and I can still feel the pain in my heart while you stand there embracing your red attire. I still can't walk up to you and tell you how I feel, I will still cry beneath the water of my washed face. I will still say that I'm okay even before you ask me and I will still ask your mother to tell you that we are with you. Maybe you don't know that I am feeling all this right now or maybe you don't know I even feel something for you and this doesn't hurt me at all. This just makes me a bit stronger, this makes me realize how, like a wall, I stood protecting you the way I could. The only pain that aches my soul is that I didn't realize when my safety boundaries changed into walls for you.

The only query this man's heart asks is when did I turn into a stone hearted father from the man who was happiest to hold his baby.

Notes I take about love

~ Whenever someone asks me the thing or the person that I love the most in the world, I start to think and think to realize nothing. I analyze everything and still I've no certain thing to point out. This greets me with certainty that love is not defined. My love for dogs is not comparable to my love for shoes. My love for going out is different from my love for staying home. My love for you is not defined. I can don't know you and still love you whereas I can know you and still love you. It's easy. It's just undefined for me. I am not capable of answering these questions to myself and sometimes it's okay. The romance with nature is a purity of love and the love for humans is generic. Having a desire to measure it with scales creates confusions. **_Don't do it._**

~The day you start loving them because they love themselves is the day when you'll actually love. I like the way you make me feel, how good you're to me, how I'm supported by you. All these are the act of selfishness you love. You don't love them. When you love them because they care to take stand for themselves, when they oppose you whenever required, when they tell you things apart from what you're used to. When in these moments of them being honest to you and to themselves, they're appreciated by you then it is the path what you are seeking for. The love you're looking for.

~Little did I know how much more I had of myself in me. How you came and added a part in me. How you made me realize I was already complete? With you or without anyone. That realization is love for me. You, are love for me. Astonished, I stare at you while you describe me. How easily you make me believe that I'm everything that you say. If I am being selfish, I'll not defend myself. How can I, when I know you're worth it all.

It is love too

~People often, in the process of protecting their loved ones, cross lines. They forget the boundaries which they wished someone had not crossed while protecting them.

Being an elder sibling, you always try to shield your younger one. To prevent from something bad happening to them. Which snatches away the right of exploring things from them. You know what you know because you took wrong decisions and you did what you did because you trusted yourself. Let your siblings trust themselves.

Let them make mistakes and let them learn.

Guide them, don't decide for them.

~ When people tell you about how they're and how they're feeling it's not always to seek attention. There might be a pure will to talk, hidden under the covers of ranting. I don't want you to listen if you can't but at least stop being stubborn about making them believe that there is no one waiting for them to talk. Play your card of being a person and just keep your silence if you can't help. Unfortunately, people struggle a lot before saying outload what the reality is and then they are slapped with stickers of " attention seekers" in the world of selfishness. This is bad. Avoid it.

When I lost you

Aren't you afraid of losing me?

The sky is burning over me and an unconditional sweat slips down my back into my pants. My arms are securing me from falling down and her eyes are the only source of anxiety that is fetching me to the guilt well. The question she asked requires an answer but my brain is singing the parody of ignorance. I can't lose what's already lost.

Her head is now slightly bent, she is sobbing, crying. This means I am right; she is here for herself not for me. She is not okay and she is seeking her okay in me but how do I tell her the truth? She decided to give up on me twice and I didn't know it, I still don't, as per her. Should I be satisfied that she chose me over everyone for her comfort or do I step back to lose the only calm I've in my life. Grabbing her arm, I stare into her brown eyes. Surprisingly they're still beautiful, I try to get hold of me but she lays her head on my heart and my sense arises. It's really hot here. She is with me, sniffing my shirt and pouring her tears on my already soaked shirt. My hands make their way and now I couldn't step back. Why do I step back? I wait for her to speak and her silence does it all. I stand there looking at our future and nothing in particular but she felt same in my arms. The lost things felt right back at place at least for now. Sorry. Sorry she says and I know she is, her heart is racing. I shake my head lazily because I am not angry, I am disappointed. I should not say anything and just let her hold for a while. Then I'll go away. Alone or with her. I've not decided yet.

A Bridged Gap

How beautiful and fortunate it is to have a friend who cares for you, who manages to uplift your mood just by being present there. The presence is not necessarily to be physical, just talking to them about crap and your life, makes it all a little easier to handle.

That is the kind of friendship everyone deserves but what if love enters in that pure sacred zone of bonding?

You all know how that feels, you all must have been there at least once in your life, when you are stuck sitting confused whether it's just a friendly affection or something stronger than that.

Eventually, when you realize that maybe just maybe it's love, maybe you are falling in love. But are they holding hands with you in that fall?

Are they into you the way you are?

You can't differentiate between the care that they show you now and the care that they showed earlier when you weren't aware of your affection for them.

Now everything is like a mixed bulk of signals to you, did she call me because she wanted to hear my voice or was it just another call?

Why didn't she text me today? Why am I the only one initiating the conversation?

Oh, just look at her smile, how can I not want to be the reason behind it?

All those regular days spent with your 'friend' feels a little magical now. There is nothing merrier than you imagining both of you together but like every story does, ruins the imagination by stamping the question of reality on it.

You are too afraid to confess your feelings and at the same time there is nothing more than you would rather choose than seeing her reaction when you tell her.

You have a fear of losing it all. Losing the best friend of yours and a fear to regret that what if she is the one?

This all keeps running in circles until one day when you tell her and the reaction you get is not fixed.

Maybe in my story she hugged me tight claiming my feelings to be real but not for her.

Maybe in my story she smiled with her crooked teeth and told me how much she wanted to hear this from me, while I adored her.

This just keeps going on until I decide to tell her. Until I decide to face one of my "maybes".

Two Separate stories. Maybe

~ The room smells of coffee, bitter but it's warm. Maa doesn't like coffee then why this smell? "We had guests today?" I asked her, who was sitting in the arm chair where she sits daily when I come from school.

Shrugging her shoulders, she refuses to acknowledge my question, you didn't make lunch maa? No answer again. Are you ignoring me?

Shut up, stop talking to me. Screams my mother. Scared? I'm not. How could I be scared of my own mother. Smiling I reach for her soft hand to touch, she pulls back in enough time to avoid any contact of skin to skin. You're angry with me? I ask she just stares at my face.

No but you'll be.

Oh, you're funny why would I be angry on you? You're my mother.

You'll be one day; she says and I smile without acknowledging the stress and burden in her words. I could not grasp it I was small, that is the only excuse I escape the truth with.

Today looking at the past, I've accepted my truth. My mother served men for their desires which world could not satisfy them with. She gave this world her body and soul, protected the world. Prevented thousands of rapes that her customers would have done. I am ashamed but not of her. I'll be angry one day she said. True. I'm angry but because she didn't tell me the truth of herself. I'm angry because she didn't tell me the house which I grew up in was a gift from one of her men, men who owned piece of her true self. I could never earn a single piece of her honest self.

~ This city is going to break my heart, again. The sun, the warmth, the breeze, everything is just the same. The same as it was on that day. The same breeze which touched my face and me realize that I was alive. The same air but just now it's not mixed with the smell of fresh blood. The metal taste is still there, I can still taste blood on the tip of my tongue. But for whatever reasons I cannot see it today. My hands are kept easily on my lap but why do they hurt, why does this feel like a trap?

They are all screaming, they are shouting words like " Justice and murder" and it's too much for my ears. I am so flummoxed.

Wait. Where are you taking me in this truck? I ask but there is no response. No one is responding to me, to my thoughts. A final stop and it all end. I'm being dragged now, I am in a room, a cell, a dark one. They are putting me behind bars. This day will be remembered forever, this day I was alive for the last time. This day was the last to make me feel something. Now it is just me. Always me.

A Note to men

I'm grateful for what things they have allowed me to do at present,

After all those years of women being tamed in cuffs, I feel blessed to have basic rights.

But what I still not understand is the men of my country, my home, my world. When still sitting at the table to eat, mothers serve them first. I still get confused when after an exhausting day at work, a woman is making tea for her man. It is not about sympathy anymore, there is more than that. Aren't men stronger than women? You told me they are, so why are they always too tired to wash utensils? I think they are not aware of their super powers yet. When asked about my success, it is more household queries which I answer than my role at my workplace. Not that I feel bad because I am not ashamed to admit that I cook my own meals or that I've kids to nurture. But when did you ask a man about his four-year-old kid, who is watching his children when he's here enjoying his life?

I wonder about all this, a lot these days. My brother isn't supposed to pour water in glasses for guests, he'll spill it. He says so. I wonder how we are so sure of putting our everything in making hope someday men learn how to wash their clothes without telling people as it's a favor on them. If at night, God forbid, I've to go somewhere, a man accompanies me, he is there to save me from another man. Am I that tempting to men? It is again a woman's fault. Men are superior for a reason. Some people born privileged; we call them men. Irrespective of how low a man is in his life; he is and will always be superior to some woman.

But again, I will not complain, I 'm grateful for men. Thanks for letting me live.

85